Dear Parent:
Your child's love of reading starts here!

Every child learns to read in a different way and at his or her own speed. Some go back and forth between reading levels and read favorite books again and again. Others read through each level in order. You can help your young reader improve and become more confident by encouraging his or her own interests and abilities. From books your child reads with you to the first books he or she reads alone, there are I Can Read Books for every stage of reading:

SHARED READING
Basic language, word repetition, and whimsical illustrations, ideal for sharing with your emergent reader

BEGINNING READING
Short sentences, familiar words, and simple concepts for children eager to read on their own

READING WITH HELP
Engaging stories, longer sentences, and language play for developing readers

READING ALONE
Complex plots, challenging vocabulary, and high-interest topics for the independent reader

ADVANCED READING
Short paragraphs, chapters, and exciting themes for the perfect bridge to chapter books

I Can Read Books have introduced children to the joy of reading since 1957. Featuring award-winning authors and illustrators and a fabulous cast of beloved characters, I Can Read Books set the standard for beginning readers.

A lifetime of discovery begins with the magical words "I Can Read!"

Visit www.icanread.com for information
on enriching your child's reading experience.

To Luke
—K.G.

To my daughter,
who loves to make bubbles
in the bath
—O.V.

I Can Read Book® is a trademark of HarperCollins Publishers.

Typography by Joe Merkel

Library of Congress Control Number: 2015956254
ISBN 978-0-06-235312-2 (hardcover) — ISBN 978-0-06-235311-5 (pbk.)

20 21 22   LSCC   15 14 13   ❖   First Edition

I Can Read!™

SHARED
My First
READING

DUCK, DUCK, DINOSAUR

BUBBLE BLAST

Written by Kallie George

Illustrated by Oriol Vidal

HARPER
An Imprint of HarperCollinsPublishers

This is Feather.

This is Flap.

And this is their brother, Spike.

It is summer.

Time for fun.

Big fun.

Small fun.

Summer fun!

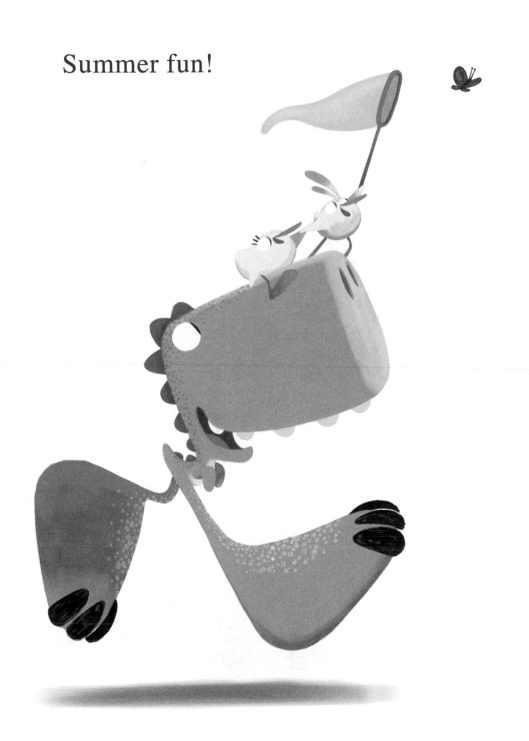

Feather, Flap, and Spike get dirty.

Very dirty.

"Time for a bath," says Mama.

"No," says Feather.

"Baths are not fun."

"No bath. No bath," says Flap.

"BATH!" says Spike.

Spike jumps into the pond.

Feather and Flap do not.

"Time for soap," says Mama.

"No," says Feather. "Soap is not fun."

"No soap. No soap," says Flap.

"SOAP!" says Spike.

Spike takes a bar of soap.

Feather and Flap do not.

"Time for scrubbing," says Mama.

"No," says Feather. "Scrubbing is not fun."

"No scrubbing. No scrubbing," says Flap.

"SCRUB!" says Spike.

Spike scrubs with a sponge.

Feather and Flap do not.

"Feather and Flap!" says Mama.

"It is time for soap.

It is time to scrub.

It is time for . . ."

"Bubbles?" asks Spike.

"Yes!" says Feather. "Bubbles are fun!"

"Yes bubbles! Yes bubbles!" says Flap.

"BUBBLES!" says Spike.

Feather and Flap jump into the pond.

Soon, bubbles are everywhere.

Big bubbles.

Small bubbles.

Bubbles are fun.

And bath time is fun, too!